W9-CFI-311

HIP-HOP
FOR dogs

FROM

BLING TO PHAT,

YOUR DOG

IS

ONE COOL

CAT

WRITTEN AND ILLUSTRATED BY

JANET PERR

SIMON & SCHUSTER

NEW YORK   LONDON   TORONTO   SYDNEY

Simon & Schuster
1230 Avenue of the Americas
New York, NY 10020

First Simon & Schuster hardcover edition November 2008

SIMON & SCHUSTER and colophon are registered
trademarks of Simon & Schuster, Inc.

For information about special discounts for bulk purchases,
please contact Simon & Schuster Special Sales at
1-800-456-6798 or business@simonandschuster.com.

Designed by Janet Perr and Jaime Putorti

Manufactured in the United States of America

10 9 8 7 6 5 4 3 2 1

Copyright © iStockphoto: p. 20, money (Stefan Klein); p. 24, doghouse (Stephen
Rees); p. 34, badge (Randolph Pamphrey); p. 58, brownstones; p. 60, car (Alija);
p. 76, martini glasses (Christine Balderas and Rafa Inusta); p. 90, chair (Geoffrey
Hammond); p. 96, motorcycle (M.E. Photographics). Copyright © Shutterstock:
p. 30, turntable (Dusan Zidar); p. 36, ice cream cone (Thomas M. Perkins); p. 70,
microphone; p. 98, boombox (Astrouskaya Alisa). Copyright © Photodisc: p. 38,
movie screen. Copyright © Stockxpert: p. 46, stuffed animal.

Library of Congress Cataloging-in-Publication Data
Perr, Janet.
Hip-hop for dogs : from bling to phat, your dog is one cool cat / written and
illustrated by Janet Perr.
p. cm.
1. Vocabulary—Humor. 2. Black English—Humor. 3. Hip hop—Humor.
4. Dogs—Humor. I. Title.
PN6231.W64P47 2008
428.102'07—dc22   2008020558
ISBN-13: 978-1-4165-9510-6
ISBN-10:   1-4165-9510-4

For Autumn,

and all the other puppies out there

who are stealing shoes,

chewing furniture,

and shredding sponges

Yo, does your dog have some *phat* sweaters? Is she a *foxy* lady? Do you spend lots of *benjamins* on your pooch? Maybe he's a *hustla,* a *playa*, or part of a *posse*. Perhaps he *chills* in your *crib* while you're *doin' a bid* at work. Possibly your canine is a *biyatch* that demands lots of *bling*. Or maybe that hound is a *ho*.

Whatever the case, you've stumbled on a fun and educational way to learn common hip-hop terms that have become part of our everyday lexicon.

Hip-hop is a genre of music that has its roots in the late '70s and early '80s in New York City. Springing from the ghetto of the South Bronx, a new form of music was born, partly as an alternative to disco and partly as an outlet for the frustrations of inner city youth. Parties were thrown where people chanted rhymes over the beats of songs (*rapping*);

manipulated sounds from vinyl records by pushing them back and forth on turntables (*scratching*); and incorporated gymnastics, martial arts, and acrobatic maneuvers to perform a physically demanding form of dance (*break dancing*). A distinctive style of dress as well as specific words, terms, and phrases emerged, all of which have been mainstreamed into modern culture over the last twenty-five years.

Hip-hop as a language is constantly changing and its slang terms are as likely to be heard on the suburban lawns of Connecticut as on the dog runs of Compton. *And our canines have been listening the whole time.* So if "*Yo,* did you *jack* that *fly* dog tag wit' da *ice* or pay mad *chedda* for that *stylin'* collar and leash?" stumps you, then perhaps your own *dawg* could tell you: "Hey, did you steal that dog tag with the diamonds or pay tons of money for that fashionable dog collar and leash?"

And when you're cruising' through *da hood* in your *tricked out* car with the *ill rims* and looking for your *homies,* remember that your pooch is back at *da crib gettin' busy wit' da fly girl* next door, and perhaps you should take him with you for a ride in *da benz,* or he'll just end up someone's *baby daddy.* After all, he's part of your *crew* and he'd rather be with you than any old *sista* from *da hood. Word.*

BABY DADDY

BAY•bee DAA•dee   *n*

Your baby's daddy, whom you did not marry, and do not even refer to as your boyfriend. In some cases you can't even remember his name. Your *baby daddy* is not involved with his child. Do not expect diapers, formula, or *chedda* from this person.

Also: *baby daddy ties,* the relationship between women who have children with the same *baby daddy*

That BABY DADDY never see any pups from his litter. He doesn't even know how many there are. He could be trotting down the street, pass one on the corner, and not even know it. They may look like him, but that doesn't mean a thing, probably jus' the same breed. They may be cute, but he don't care! That BABY DADDY'S useless and a waste of my time . . . and my mamma's time too.

BENJAMIN

BEN•jah•min   *n*

A one-hundred-dollar bill. Benjamin Franklin's face is on the front of the hundred-dollar bill. He was a Founding Father of the United States, a scientist, inventor, statesman, and diplomat.

Also: *C-note* (from the Roman numeral for 100)

I found this BENJAMIN while I was eating my owner's wallet. You can be sure that I'll be bustin' through the hole in the fence later and takin' myself to the pet store. I'm sure all the *dawgs* in the *hood* will follow me. That's *aight,* I'll get them their favorite treats. And me? I think I'll pick myself up a *bling bling* dog tag with my name inscribed in *ice* on it. I been eyein' that puppy for a while now.

BENZ

bends   *n*

Short for Mercedes Benz, a German luxury car company. If you want to look your finest, you drive a *Benz,* 'specially when it's got *tricked out* rims.

When I hear "*Yo,* ya *down* for a ride in the car?" I grab my leash and run to the door, tail wagging. I love cruising around the *hood* in the BENZ lookin' out for my *peeps.* Windows open, snout in the air, wind in my face, that's one *dope* way to spend the afternoon in style.

BIYATCH

BEE•atch   *n*

1. Derived from "bitch" though not quite as mean-spirited

2. A mean female, or a diva

3. Often used in reference to an ex-wife or ex-girlfriend or, in some cases, one's *baby mamma*

I came outta my building to see all these *homies* hangin' near my favorite hydrant. "Be out, *dawgs*!" I screeched. "I don't need *yo* sorry selves blocking the entrance to my *crib*."

"Chill, BIYATCH," they barked back. "You don't have to be so nasty. We're waitin' for the dog walker . . . who jus' happens to live in your building!"

BLING

Bleeng   *n*

1. A flashy or gaudy piece of jewelry.

2. *Bling* can be expensive, such as gold and diamonds, but is sometimes not, and is worn to give the impression of wealth. Usually, the more *bling*, the bigger the ego of the wearer.

When I'm hangin' wit' my *crew* in the *dawg* run, I rock my BLING. A leather collar or simple chain? Nah! I got my BLING, I hold my snout in the air, and all the other *dawgs* know who da leader of da pack is.

BLUNT

bluhnt   *n*

A cigar that has been emptied out and refilled with marijuana. The term *blunt* comes from Phillies Blunts, a cigar brand that was originally used for this purpose, though any brand of cigar will do.

Similar: *spliff,* a marijuana cigarette

Yo, dawg, pass that BLUNT. My owner won't be back for a few hours and I know if he gets his hands on that *thang* he'll forget to take me out for my late-night walk. And that would be *wack*! Might as well be me who's *illin'.*

BOOTY

BOO•tee   *n*

Buttocks, butt, rear end, derriere, bottom. Most often *booty* is used to describe the rear end of a female.

Also: *badonkadonk*: a very large and round booty

I used to think my BOOTY was a liability. It was kinda large compared to the rest of me. But when all the *brothas* started following me home, I thought, *Hmmmm, this could turn out to be my greatest asset* (no pun intended!).

BREAK DANCE

BRAKE•dants   *v*

To engage in a physically demanding form of dance,
originating from the streets of New York City in the late
1970s, and accompanied by the rhythmic beats of early rap
and hip-hop music. Dancers perform innovative routines to
remixed beats, often using upper-body strength to execute
gymnastic-like moves.

Related: *B-boy* and *B-girl*, people who *break dance.*

You probably didn't think an old *dawg* like me could still
busta move and BREAK DANCE. Well, I been doin' my
power moves since I was a pup. I can still throw my hind legs
up over my head. But when I'm done, I be catchin' some
ZZZZs for the rest of the afternoon.

BUSTED

BUSS•tid *adj*

Ugly, referring to a female that no self-respecting *homie* will go near

Also: *fugly,* from *fu*#in' ugly*

Some of the boys in the *hood* may call me BUSTED, but don't feel sorry for me. I know that my eyes are crossed, my ears have no hair, I need orthodontia, and I only have three legs. So what! I'm a *fly-ass foxy lady* on the inside. Who needs those loser *homies* anyhow?

CHEDDA

CHEDD•ah   *n*

Money, and lots of it. Piles of money, not just a few bucks

Related words: *scrilla* (money), *fresh cheese* (new money)

I got me some CHEDDA, so I'll be going to the pet store on the corner for some squeaky toys and organic treats. And that $350 red velvet dog bed with the gold tassels in the window? That's gonna be mine too. *Dawg* shampoo, Poochi collars with matching leashes . . . not a problem. And on my way home, I'll be stoppin' at the butcher for some filet mignon . . . or maybe a porterhouse.

CHILL

chil   *v*

1. To relax, to take it easy

2. To calm down, to cool off

3. To hang out

Also: *chillax,* to chill and relax

After a long afternoon chasing my *homies* at the dog run, I like to come back to the *crib* and lie in my favorite spot, the square of sun that moves slowly across the kitchen floor. It gets crazy out there sometimes . . . the whole *crew* runnin' around nippin' at each other, chasin' balls, and diggin' holes. A *brotha* needs to CHILL after a day like that.

CRIB

krib   *n*

1. Your house, your home

2. A place of residence

I'm the king of the castle when it comes to my CRIB. No one's tellin' me what to do. No "Fetch!" No "Sit!" And no "Stay!" No other *dawgs* sniffin' and nippin'. I just *chill* and enjoy the peace and quiet in a place I call my own.

CRISTAL

Kris•STAHL   *n*

An opulent champagne for the well-heeled and moneyed, often mentioned in rap songs. You're living large if you drink *Cristal,* which often costs $500 per bottle.

Also: *Cris, Crissy*

We was out one night, me and my owner, at the hottest spot in *da hood.* Yeah, they let all the *phat dawgs* in. Well, the waiter brings over a bottle of CRISTAL—I couldn't believe it, but my owner was *down* with it. I figured I'd put on my shades so I could look *fresh* sippin' my CRISTAL. To tell you the truth, a bowl of water would've been fine with me.

DA BOMB

Duh•BOMM   *n*

1. The best, the most fabulous

2. Something or someone that is really cool, amazing

Look at me—I'm hot and I dress fine. None of those cruddy old dog sweaters for me. I go to the groomer, I'm *stylin'*, I look *mad fly,* and the otha *dawgs* follow my tail all day itchin' for a sniff. I'm cute, I'm popular, I'm DA BOMB.

DJ

DEE•jaye *n*

1. Short for disc jockey

2. A person who spins records creating new rhythms and beats through scratching and mixing

3. The record spinner at a party or nightclub responsible for keeping people on the dance floor having a great time

---

That party out on the street last night was insane. The whole block was there. With the DJ spinnin', my owner was dancing till all hours. Everyone was outside—eating, drinking, and *bustin'* some *phat* moves. Us *dawgs* had the best time, though—all that food droppin' on the street is more fun than groovin' to some beats.

DOIN' A BID

DO•in a BID   *v*

Spending time in jail or prison

Also: *at school, goin' upstate, down South*

My owners went off on vacation and here I am DOIN' A BID at the doggy day care. They said it would be fun, but, *yo,* who wants to exercise on a treadmill, and then play fetch with a bunch of strange *dawgs*? The worst part is now I've got this kennel cough. I tell ya, I'd much rather be in the *hood chillin' wit' da crew.*

FIVE-O

Five•OH   *n*

The police, the cops, the fuzz, the pigs. From the TV show
Hawaii Five-O, about the Hawaii state police department.

Also: *5-0, Feds, the popo*

When I walk down the street, all the *dawgs* better be droppin'
the bootleg stuff in their mouths. You wouldn't believe what
they pick up: tissues, bottle caps, stones. But they see the
FIVE-O roundin' the corner and they drop it, or they end up
getting yanked by the *popo* and thrown in the *dawg* pound.

FLAVA

FLAY•vuh   *n*

1. From the word *flavor*

2. Style or personality

Look at me, *yo,* I'm *stylin'* just like my idol, FLAVOR FLAV.
He's got *mad wicked* FLAVA in more ways than one. That
bling, the *grills,* he's *phat.* And forget those bully sticks and
liver FLAVA-ed dog treats back at my *crib,* I got my favorite
FLAVAS right here.

FLICK

flik   *n*

Movie

Yo, goin' out and catchin' a FLICK with my *peeps* is a fine way to spend a Saturday night. I don't like the slasher FLICKS, and the love stories are *wack.* Actually, I don't care what's on the screen—I'm too busy with all the popcorn that falls on the floor.

FLY

fliy *adj*

Hip, cool, in style, good looking

Step off my tail, *bro,* you're *wack,* you got no style, you're not even a handsome *dawg*! You have no right to go sniffin' around a FLY-ass *biyatch* such as myself. Go home!

FOXY

FOCKS•ee   *adj*

A hot babe, a beautiful young woman, a fine piece of ass.
Attractive, sexy, a real hottie

Also: *foxy lady*

Mmmm, mmm . . . all the *dawgs* on the block be sniffin' me
and following me around. I'm the hottest lady in the *hood*
with my long legs and sexy 'do. The *dawgs* are always standing
by my *crib,* waiting for this FOXY lady to make an
appearance. I love the attention . . . and I get the pick of
the litter!

GANGSTA

GANG•stah   *n, adj*

1. As a noun, *gangsta* is from the word gangster, a tough guy, a criminal, one who dabbles in illegal activity.

2. As an adjective, the word *gangsta* can be used to describe the appearance or attitude of someone trying to be tough but who is not necessarily a bad guy.

Also: *thug*

Yo, I may stand on the corner lookin' all tough and scary, but I ain't no GANGSTA. I'm a good *dawg*. It's all just fashion to me. I'm really just a big softy who loves to be scratched behind the ears and have my belly rubbed. *Word.*

GET BUSY

get BIZZ•eee   *v*

To have sex

Same as: *do the nasty, the freak, the wild thing*

The cute bichon down the street? Who needs her? I be GETTIN' BUSY with my owner's leg, my dog bed, the baby's fluffy toy, and the pillows on the couch. And if I see the bichon, that's just icing on the cake.

GHETTO

GEH•toe   *adj, n*

1. Something of poor quality: cheap, chintzy, crummy, or outdated; something that was slapped together haphazardly

2. A specific area of a city inhabited by a concentrated population of the same minority, often poor and part of the underclass

---

When I cruise through my *hood* hunting for treasures, I'm hopin' to find something *dope* like a Chinese food container with the remnants of pork fried rice. But I usually come up with *wack* crap. Today I found a filthy old ripped T-shirt, some food wrappers, and the broken inner workings of a GHETTO VCR with the tape still in it . . . all of which I dragged home and buried behind my *crib*.

GRAFFITI

Grah•FEE•tee *n*

Markings or inscriptions, lettering or images, usually on public property. Graffiti can range from a simple Magic Marker tag of someone's initials to a complicated full-color wall mural done in spray paint. Some regard it as art—to others, it's vandalism.

All the *dawgs* know when I been by they *crib*. I leave my *tag* in a beautiful and artistic manner. I could mark my territory in other ways, but GRAFFITI is much nicer!

GRILLS

grilz   *n*

1. Gold or silver caps that fit over your teeth, sometimes with diamonds *(iced out)*

2. *Bling* for the mouth

Also: *fronts, grillz*

Nothing helps my *fugly* self. I'll never be *stylin'* or *phat*! Maybe I should let my hair grow out instead of walking around with this *wack* 'do. These *fresh* GRILLS should help too. Got to be careful with the rawhide bone, though, I don't want to wreck this *bling*.

HO

hoe   *n*

1. Short for whore, but more lighthearted. A female who is slutty, who *gets busy* with multiple partners

2. Or a female who just looks like she's *busy* with everyone in the *hood*

It's not that I'm a HO, I jus' like messin' around with the *dawgs* in the *hood* and lookin' fine. I do look fine, don't I? If you meet me at the run after your morning walk, I'll hook up with you.

HOMIES

HOE•mees   *n*

1. Friends, buddies, pals

2. Usually good friends from the same street or neighborhood (*hood*) that have known each other a long time or have grown up together

Also: *homey, homegirl, homeboy, sista, brotha, bro*

My HOMIES and I have known each other since obedience school. We roll through the *hood* together, we hang in the dog run together, we hunt for leftovers together, and we check out the *sistas* together. We'll always run in the same pack, best friends forever.

HOOD

hood *n*

Short for neighborhood, the area where you live or grew up

We all grew up on this block and we'll never leave it. We love it, it's our home. All our *peeps* are here, all *da dawgs,* our *cribs.* We've sniffed every crack in the street, peed on every fire hydrant, chased each other at the dog run, and *jacked* treats from the pet store. We got everything we need, here in our HOOD.

HOOPTIE

HOOP•tee   *n*

A beat-up old car, usually an unfashionable late-model sedan.
It still runs but the tailpipe's dragging on the ground, the
radio's broken, it's rusted, and it has numerous dents. Not
even *phat rims* will help this *ride*.

I'm just chillin' on this HOOPTIE that's parked in front of
my *crib*. The sun hits it all day long; it's a *dope* place to hang.
Of course, you would never see me cruisin' the streets in this
old *wack* hunk o'junk. This *ride* won't get me any *street
cred* . . . after all, it ain't no *Benz*.

HUSTLA

HUSS•lah   *n*

1. Short for hustler

2. Someone who is good at making money at a particular endeavor, whether legal or illegal

---

I got my dog-walkin' business going just fine. I let all the *dawgs* out of their *cribs* after their owners leave for work. They run around the *hood* in a frenzy all day while I'm *kickin' it* in the sun and counting my *scrilla*. Then I put them back in their *cribs*, exhausted, and they're the perfect *chillaxin'* pets when their owners return. I'm a real HUSTLA.

ICE

EYE•sss   *n*

Diamonds

No leather dog collar for me. No bone-shaped, state-issued dog license dangling from my neck. No ratty old leash. And certainly no *ghetto* harness. It's just ICE and *bling* all the way for this *brotha*.

JACK

jak   *v*

To steal, to rip someone off, to take from either a store or a
person

Synonym: *gank*

I JACKED those treats, I JACKED that rawhide chew toy,
and now they're mine! You want them back? Forget it—I be
workin' that hide for at least an hour. And those tasty treats?
I'll be buryin' those babies in the yard for *lata*.

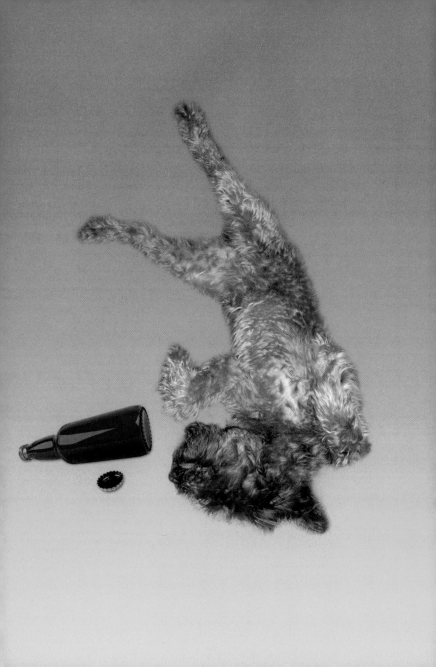

KRUNK

kruhnk

Crazy drunk, inebriated to the point of being completely trashed, plastered

Also spelled *crunk.*

My owner is *wack,* he spilled his *forty* on the floor and was too KRUNK to pick it up. Well, I didn't know what it was, but I did what I always do when people food or drink comes my way—I lapped it up *with the quickness.* Next thing I know I'm also KRUNKED outta my mind. And in the morning? *Yo,* I couldn't even chase a tennis ball, my head was so messed up.

MC

em•SEE   *n*

1. Master of Ceremonies or Mic Controller: most likely
Jamaican in origin

2. Someone who is in control of the microphone, the host
of an event

Also: *emcee*

Me and my *brothas* had a great time at the jam last night. It
was *mad chill*—lots of *foxy* bitches, plenty of kibble, and I
kept the *dawgs* groovin' in style way into the night with my
freestyle rhymes. I was the *freshest* MC the animal shelter ever
had at one of their benefits.

PHAT

fat *adj*

1. Stylish, cool, awesome

2. Originally an acronym for *Pretty Hot And Tempting*

Yo, check it out, I'm one PHAT *dawg.* Got my *stylin'* shades, got my *flava,* but most of all I got my attitude. It's that 'tude that keeps me bein' the leader of the pack. No one's gonna mess with me.

PIMP

pimp   *n*

1. One whose business it is to control a ring of prostitutes

2. Something ultracool or *tricked out*

I ain't no PIMP, really, I'm just a little dude tryin' to impress the *foxy sistas.* Of course, it's really not working too well. They just think I'm a little *dawg* with a big hat. Guess it's time to try some new tricks.

PLAYA

PLAY•ya   *n*

In the hierarchy of males, the *playa* is at the top. Ego-driven and successful, he always gets the hot girls.

Related: *playa hata*—one who is jealous of a *playa* and his expert skills in handling women and business

---

The top *dawg,* that's me. I got the *fly biyatches.* I got plenty of *chedda,* and a *phat crib.* They call me a real PLAYA, but I don't know, I'm just a *homie* from *da hood* who was "best in show." Since then, all the *sistas* be *sweatin'* me everywhere I go.

POSSE

POSS•eee   *n*

1. A group of friends that you hang out with

2. An entourage, a clique

This is my POSSE, all kinds of *dawgs,* all shapes and sizes.
They're my friends. We hang together, chasin' balls, runnin'
in the park. We watch each other's backs—safety in numbers,
ya know. And we have our internal hierarchy, da pooch code.
After all, we're pack animals.

RAP

rapp

1. *n* A music genre that features rhymes spoken over dance rhythms, dating from the late 1970s and early '80s

2. *v* To speak rhymes over dance beats in a musical and heartfelt way

---

Sit, stay . . . no way! We rhyme to beats and walk this way. You may be *illin'* but we be *thrillin'*. We the kings of RAP, and take no crap. They say it's tricky but we ain't picky. We got the beat, we from the street, and it sure is sweet.

REPRESENT

rep•ree•ZENT   *v*

To show where you come from (either geographically or personally), to show your roots with pride. It's usually used as an exclamation: *"Represent!"*

My *homie* moved to LA and he started actin' all West Side and everything. I said, "*Yo,* come back to the city—what you wanna be peeing on palm trees for? Plus, you'll never find a leftover corned-beef sandwich in the garbage there." *Brotha,* this is the greatest city in the world. *Yo,* REPRESENT!

RIMS

rimmz *n*

The car wheel (not the tire). *Rims* are often customized to show off status.

Related: *dubs, spinners*

My owner got some *phat* RIMS on his *Benz*. One time, the dumbest *dawg* on the block ran right into the RIMS when the *Benz* was parked out front cuz the *dubs* was so shiny, he thought it was another *dawg* to play with. What a fool.

SHORTY

SHORE•dee   *n*

1. Your girlfriend

2. A pretty female who is well-liked

3. An attractive girl that you would like to date

I hear "*Yo,* SHORTY" and I come runnin'. I know it's my main *B-boy* callin' me. We go sniffing 'round the *hood,* we dig holes, we look for tasty tidbits of food that dropped on the street, and we hang in the run together. Maybe one day he'll be my boyfriend.

SISTA

SISS•tah   *n*

1. A dignified black woman who is proud of her heritage

2. A female friend

Related: *girlfriend*

Me and my homegirls, we stick together everywhere we go: at the groomer gettin' our 'dos, on the street sniffin' the *B-boys,* and all over the *hood* avoidin' the *baby daddies.* Some of us are *busted,* some of us are *fly,* some got small *bootys,* some have *badonkadonks.* But all of us run in the same pack, help each other, and watch out for each other's pups. I don't know what I'd do without my SISTAS.

STYLIN'

STIY•linn   *v*

Stylish, looking sharp

I'm one *phat brotha.* No matter where I go, no matter what I do, I'm STYLIN'. I read *Dogue* and get all my 'quipment— the leashes, beds, sweaters, and bowls—from the high-class stores where the *dawgs* with real *chedda* shop. I got the attitude that matters and the *pimpin'* threads that flatter. *Yo, shorty,* c'mere!

'SUP

supp   *interj*

1. An abbreviated version of "*What's up?*" meaning "What's happening?" or "What's going on?"

2. A greeting meaning "hello"

Related: *what-up*

"'SUP, *dawg*?"
"Jus' chillin', 'SUP wit' you?"
"Nothin' much."
"I'm outta here, *aight*?"
"*Lata.*"

TIMBS

tims   *n*

Timberland shoes. (Timberland is a manufacturer of rugged, premium-quality shoes and boots, as well as luggage, apparel, and accessories).

I love to steal shoes and drag them all around the house. When my owner goes to work I chew up his slippers, fling the flip-flops around the living room, toss the Adidas down the hallway, and drag the TIMBS to my bed. I guess you could say I have a foot fetish.

TRICKED OUT

Trikt•OWT   *adj*

1. Extravagantly accessorized

2. Altered in an elaborate way with either visual or performance-enhancing modifications

Also: *pimped out*

My owner's got this TRICKED OUT bike that's *da bomb*. He parks it out front of the *crib* and I hop on when he's not looking. I wish I could cruise through the *hood* on this puppy, but I'm afraid of the loud noise comin' outta that *pimped out* motor. So I'll just sit here, wag my tail, perk my ears, and look *phat* instead.

WACK

wak   *adj*

1. Out of style

2. Crummy, of low quality

I was tryin' to bring the late '80s and early '90s back. It was a cool time, some *ill* styles. But it ain't workin'. My *crew* tells me I'm WACK. They want no part of it. They don't even want to be seen with me in the park. I guess I ain't *stylin'* enough to be startin' any new trends.

YO

yoe *interj*

1. A greeting meaning "hi"

2. A word used to get your attention, similar to "hey"

3. Short for "your," as in *yo mama*

Yo is most often used at the beginning or end of a sentence for emphasis, but can also be inserted in the middle for no apparent reason.

YO, what up, *bro*? I got YO *bling* on my collar. Remember you lent it to me? Take it back, YO, it's heavy and clunky. Where'd you put my regular collar, YO? Did you bury it behind YO *crib*? That ain't cool, YO!

ACKNOWLEDGMENTS

Special thanks to David Rosenthal, one of the funniest people I know, and Kerri Kolen, who's *da bomb.*

Many thanks to my friend Pam, who set me straight about the difference between a *blunt* and a *spliff,* informed me that *at school* did not involve books, and let me know that *timbs* were not *chuckas.* I'd also like to thank John and Anna for answering my endless questions about what's *wack* and what's not.

In particular, I'd like to *give props* to Jordan for his Mac expertise, and Harvey for *chillin'* and letting me work.

A *high-five* to all the *dawgs* who were *chill* enough to participate in this book. Some were *phat,* some were *wack,* and some didn't want to be pulled away from their *posse.* I photographed the *hotties* and the *fuglies,* and everything in between. And of course, all were given lots of treats and praised, whether they were *chillaxin'* or running around *jackin'* old socks, *fo' shizzle*:

Abby, Ally, Amelia, Annie, Archie, Autumn, Banjo, Bear, Bella, Betty, Billy, Bonnie, Bruno, Buddy, Buster, Chou Chou, Cooper, Daisy, Dottie, Elliot, Ernie, Freddy, Friendly, Fritz, Hank, Happy, Henry, Imus, Jazmin, Kaylee, Keiko, Libby, Louie, Luke, Mikey, Monster, Mowgli, Murphy, Nike, Nuri, Ozzie, Pepe, Raven, Rita, Rockford, Rosie, Sadie, Scooter, Sebastian, Shally, Six, Sky, Smokey, Sonnie, Sonny, Sophie, Spice, Suzy, Taja, and Toby.